Rescue and Shelter Dogs

Alex Summers

Rourke
Educational Media

rourkeeducationalmedia.com

Scan for Related Titles
and Teacher Resources

Before Reading:

Building Academic Vocabulary and Background Knowledge

Before reading a book, it is important to tap into what your child or students already know about the topic. This will help them develop their vocabulary, increase their reading comprehension, and make connections across the curriculum.

1. *Look at the cover of the book. What will this book be about?*
2. *What do you already know about the topic?*
3. *Let's study the Table of Contents. What will you learn about in the book's chapters?*
4. *What would you like to learn about this topic? Do you think you might learn about it from this book? Why or why not?*
5. *Use a reading journal to write about your knowledge of this topic. Record what you already know about the topic and what you hope to learn about the topic.*
6. *Read the book.*
7. *In your reading journal, record what you learned about the topic and your response to the book.*
8. *After reading the book complete the activities below.*

Content Area Vocabulary
Read the list. What do these words mean?

adopted
exercise
euthanized
facility
fostered
neutering
organizations
relinquished
spaying
volunteer

After Reading:

Comprehension and Extension Activity

After reading the book, work on the following questions with your child or students in order to check their level of reading comprehension and content mastery.

1. *Explain the difference between fostering a dog and adopting a dog. (Summarize)*
2. *Can rabies affect humans? Explain. (Asking Questions)*
3. *What are some ways you can help your local rescue or shelter? (Text to self connection)*
4. *Why is it important to visit a shelter a few times when looking for a dog? (Summarize)*
5. *Why are volunteers an important part of rescues and shelters? (Asking Questions)*

Extension Activity
Raise awareness! Write a persuasive essay on why you should adopt a dog from a rescue or shelter. Research and visit your local animal shelter or rescue and talk with the people who volunteer. Research facts on the Internet from reliable sources such as The Humane Society. Then share your essay with your classmates, parents, or local newspaper.

Table of Contents

Chapter 1

What is a Dog Rescue?

Have you ever heard of a dog rescue? A dog rescue takes in abused or neglected dogs, or dogs that are surrendered by their owners. They also take in dogs that are in danger of being **euthanized** in an animal shelter.

FURRY FACT

Low adoption rates are one factor driving the high number of animals in shelters. Another factor is the millions of dogs relinquished by their owners or rescued from the streets by private rescue organizations. These circumstances leave shelters and rescue groups with a large number of animals in need of homes.

Most communities have several dog rescues. Some rescues focus on certain breeds of dogs while others take in all breeds. Rescue **organizations** like this one called, The Dog Liberator, located in Central Florida, rescues and transports dogs. They rely solely on donations and volunteers to care for the dogs until they are **adopted**.

Since 2009, The Dog Liberator has rescued, rehabilitated, spayed or neutered, and re-housed over 900 dogs throughout the Southeast! Gisele Veilleux is the president and founder of The Dog Liberator.

Gisele Veilleux is an advocate for the well-being of animals, especially dogs.

FURRY FACT

The Dog Liberator is a non-profit organization dedicated to rescuing homeless and abandoned dogs, primarily dogs from high-kill shelters and owners who can no longer care for them. By working with committed volunteers, local veterinarians, trainers, and foster homes, they are able to rescue hundreds of dogs every year. To learn more about The Dog Liberator visit their website at www.thedogliberator.com

Veterinarians will often take care of the dogs without charging money just to make sure they get the proper care they need.

After being rescued the dog is sent to a veterinarian to be tested for diseases like heartworms, rabies, parvo, or signs of neglect or abuse.

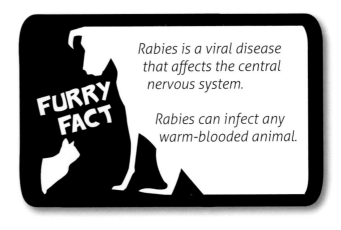

FURRY FACT

Rabies is a viral disease that affects the central nervous system.

Rabies can infect any warm-blooded animal.

They also check to see if the animal has been spayed or neutered, and if they have a microchip or tattoo that could identify the owner.

The dog is then **fostered**, or sent to live with a **volunteer** who works with the rescue. These volunteers may work for more than one rescue at a time and have more than one dog at a time. A foster plays an important role in learning about the dog's temperament, and how well they get along with other animals or children making it easier for the dog to find a forever home.

Fostering is one of the biggest roles in a rescue organization. It takes a lot of time and love but the return you get is well worth it!

Fostering more than one dog can be a challenge but it often helps the dog integrate back into a family or pack.

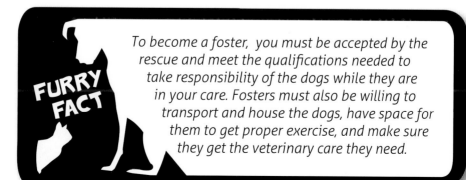

FURRY FACT

To become a foster, you must be accepted by the rescue and meet the qualifications needed to take responsibility of the dogs while they are in your care. Fosters must also be willing to transport and house the dogs, have space for them to get proper exercise, and make sure they get the veterinary care they need.

Chapter 2
What is a Dog Shelter?

A shelter is a **facility** where animals are housed until they can find new homes, or can be returned to their owners. Every year in the United States 7.6 million animals enter shelters with 3.9 million of those being dogs.

Animal shelters can be categorized in three different ways: municipal animal shelters that are run by city or county governments, private non-profit shelters that are overseen by a board of directors, and private non-profit shelters with a government contract that act to provide animal control services.

Shelters try and provide dogs with the proper exercise they need but with overcrowding and a lack of volunteers, it is sometimes difficult and the dogs are caged most of the time.

FURRY FACT

The first animal shelters were created in New York in 1894 after the first anti-animal cruelty laws were approved. Today, The Humane Society of the United States is the nation's largest and most effective animal protection organization.

Some shelters have a no-kill policy, which means they will keep the dogs until they are adopted. But sadly, some shelters are so over crowded they cannot keep the dogs for the necessary time it may take to find a new owner. In these cases the dogs are euthanized, or put to sleep.

FURRY FACT

Approximately 1.2 million dogs are euthanized each year in the U.S. Many strays are lost pets who were not kept properly indoors or provided with identification.

■ 1.4 million dogs are adopted from shelters each year in the U.S.

■ 542,000 shelter dogs are returned to their owners each year in the U.S.

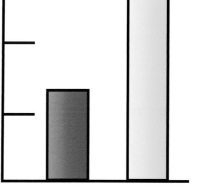

- Approximately twice as many dogs enter shelters as strays compared to the number that are **relinquished**, or given up, by their owners.

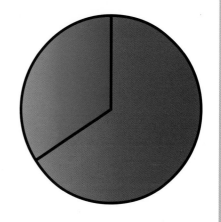

■ dogs entering shelter as strays
■ dogs that are relinquished

Source: ASPCA

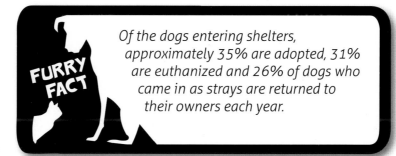

FURRY FACT

Of the dogs entering shelters, approximately 35% are adopted, 31% are euthanized and 26% of dogs who came in as strays are returned to their owners each year.

Chapter 3
What is the Solution?

Owning a dog is a long-term commitment. Some people don't think of the responsibilities and time it takes to care for a dog when they purchase or adopt one. The love, attention, **exercise**, and proper medical care a dog needs can become too much for some people to handle in today's busy world.

Dogs need a lot of attention and need to feel loved and needed, just like you!

Doc Holiday and Wyatt Earp, rescued by The Dog Liberator are packed and ready to be adopted.

No one can resist the face of a cute puppy in a pet store. Adopting a puppy or dog from a rescue or shelter can help save the life of an animal who may have no other chance. Most rescue animals make great companion, agility, and special needs dogs. About 25 percent of shelter animals are purebreds.

When looking for the best dog for your family, be sure to do your research. If you are adopting from a rescue, you may ask for a private visit, or meet, with the dog or dogs that the volunteer is fostering. Chances are, you will find your special match!

If you are adopting from a shelter, make sure you walk through more than once so you won't miss any furry faces you might not have seen the first time. You can ask to have a private visit with the dog so you can see how it interacts with you and your family members.

Jax was one of four puppies rescued by The Dog Liberator. Two of his siblings were blind. By meeting one on one with him, he found his forever home.

Spaying or **neutering** your dog helps control the pet population and ensures that the number of unwanted, abandoned, and surrendered dogs can be controlled. It can also prevent a litter of unexpected puppies!

Spaying or neutering your dog can be done in a single day, with little aftercare. The cost is minimal or is often included in the adoption fee.

Chapter 4
Before You Adopt!

Remember, take your time. Unfortunately, rescues and shelters take in dogs every day so come back if you don't find the dog for you. It just takes that one face to know, this is the one!

Checklist

Use this checklist to see if adopting a rescue or shelter dog is the right decision for you.

- ☑ *Do I have time to exercise a dog?*
- ☑ *Can I afford the medical costs for a dog?*
- ☑ *Do I have the attention to give to a dog?*
- ☑ *Do I have the right environment for a dog to live in?*
- ☑ *Do I have the commitment it takes to make a dog a part of my family?*

By adopting a rescue or shelter dog, like this one named Mr. Beans, rescued by The Dog Liberator, you are saving the life of an innocent animal who will be a loyal, loving companion.

Mr. Beans deserves a forever home.

FURRY FACT

Pets can ease loneliness, reduce stress, promote social interaction, encourage exercise and playfulness, and provide unconditional love and affection. Caring for a pet may even help you live longer.

Now that you know more about rescue and shelter dogs, you can decide if this is the right decision for you and your family. You will enjoy the love that only a dog can give!

Dundee, adopted June 2014 from Aussie And Me.

Carter adopted Kimber Rose in June 2014 from the Mundelein Police Department.

Summer adopted Jax from The Dog Liberator in May 2013.

Louis adopted Lucy in February 2011 at the Pet Palooza event sponsored through The Humane Society of Tampa Bay.

Ruby was adopted in December, 2013 from Royal Potcake Rescue in Atlanta, Georgia. She was born in Abaco Bahamas.

Ralph was adopted from the SPCA of Luzerne County in 2009.

Owning a rescue or shelter dog will be one of the best decisions your family has ever made!

It is the goal of all rescue organizations and animal shelters to adopt out as many of their animals as possible to loving homes. They attempt to keep the cost of adopting down and the fee often includes shots and spaying or neutering. The fee differs with each rescue or shelter. Rescues and shelters are very careful who they allow to adopt an animal.

A dog will always give you the love and attention you need and it's always nice to have someone so happy to see you on the other side of the door.

Some have a long application process, often including references and mandatory home visits.

How Can You Help?

Do careful research on the type, size, and temperament of the dog you are looking for.

Check your local area for any rescue or shelters before buying from a pet store.

Donate your time or extra money you save to an organization that you feel needs help.

Tell your friends and family about the importance of spaying and neutering their pets.

Do a research paper, opinion paper, or science project giving facts on rescue and shelter dogs.

If you find a stray dog, make sure to take it to your nearest shelter or veterinarian to see if it has a microchip or tattoo that may give information on the owner.

Organize a food drive at your school and collect food and other supplies that you can donate to a local rescue or shelter.

Glossary

adopted (uh-DOP-tid): to take by choice into your home or life

exercise (ex-uhr-SIZE): physical activity that is done in order to become stronger and healthier

euthanized (yu-the-NIZED): subject to euthanasia; put to sleep permanently

facility (fah-sil-uh-tee): something that is built or established to serve a particular purpose

fostered (fah-stuhrd): to have provided care

neutering (NOO-tuhr-een): removing the reproductive organs in a male animal

organizations (or-guh-ni-ZAY-shuhns): companies or businesses that are formed for a particular reason

relinquished (ruh-leen-kwishd): to withdraw or leave behind

spaying (SPAY-ing): removing the reproductive organs in a female animal

volunteer (vah-luhn-teer): a person who does work without getting paid

Index

Show What You Know

1. How many dogs are euthanized each year in the United States?
2. Why is it important to meet with a dog prior to rescuing or adopting?
3. What is one way you can raise awareness about rescuing or adopting a dog?
4. What is the difference between a rescue and a shelter facility?
5. Why is spaying or neutering a dog so important?

Websites to Visit

thedogliberator.com/about-us
www.humanesociety.org
theanimalrescuesite.greatergood.com

About the Author

Alex Summers is a true animal lover. Over the years she has had everything from dogs, horses, cats, ducks, rabbits, birds, and even snakes! With two daughters, she feels like animals are not only a learning experience for kids, but a necessary part of growing up. By the way, the snake was not her favorite! She lives in Florida where there are, unfortunately, plenty of slithering snakes!

Meet The Author!
www.meetREMauthors.com

PHOTO CREDITS: Cover: ©Oliveshadow; cover (middle): ©Suhipan Yakham; title page, page 5, page 13, page 14, page 17: ©The Dog Liberator; page 4: ©Anton Gvozdikov; page 6: ©markhatfield; page 7: ©gorillaimages; page 8: ©Eric Isselee; page9: ©mouse_sonya; page10: ©VlLevi; page 12: ©hartcreations; page 15: ©apenrock; page 17: ©monkeybusiness; page 18: ©Rourke Educational Media; page 19: ©Andres Rodriguez; page 20: ©Albany Pictures; page 21 (top): ©rofoto; page 21 (middle): ©Joana lopes; page 21 (middle): ©xalanx; page 21 (bottom): ©Radu Bercan

Edited by: Luana Mitten

Cover and Interior design by: Jen Thomas

Library of Congress PCN Data

Rescue and Shelter Dogs / Alex Summers
(Animal Matters)
ISBN 978-1-63430-064-3 (hard cover)
ISBN 978-1-63430-094-0 (soft cover)
ISBN 978-1-63430-120-6 (e-Book)
Library of Congress Control Number: 2014953368

Also Available as:

Printed in the United States of America, North Mankato, Minnesota